Poetic Darkness: When Writing is Better than Dying

Bernadette Henderson

BookLeaf Publishing

India | USA | UK

Presentation by *BookLeaf Publishing*

Web: www.bookleafpub.com

E-mail: info@bookleafpub.com

ISBN: 9789360940256

First edition 2024

This labor of insanity is dedicated to the loves I lost along the way; My first and forever I Do, my late husband Arnold Henderson. My best friend Tony McLean. Thank you for always seeing me in all my imperfections. My dad, Dallas Toles Jr. I know you did the best that you could. A man raising a daughter. I'm glad we grew together. My Mother, Delores Pearman Lindsay. Thank you for always being there for me, even when you weren't able. I Love you all in this life and the next.

ACKNOWLEDGEMENT

I was introduced to slam poets such as Jessica Care-Moore whose poems read like black anthems that demanded female empowerment. In her poem, "Warriors Walk Alone," she says, "Black girls are dying cause no one showed us how to live. Such a simple statement has so much power in it. It's hard to live when you're always in survival mode.   Then there's the teacher and poet, Taylor Mali, whose verses impart life lessons. In his poem, "Like Lilly Like Wilson", he lets the reader know that it's okay to challenge your own understanding of the world around you, especially when there is new information presented or your current understanding is not based on facts. When a student is not able to find resources to support her views, about homosexuality and determines she must change her thinking, he writes, "And I want to tell her to do more than just believe it, /but to enjoy it! /That changing your mind is one of the best ways/of finding out whether or not you still have one." Another poet that I enjoy is Beau Sia. Like Maya Angelou, he embraces his Asian Heritage and the racial stereotypes, attributed to Asians. His poetry has a comedic spin on life situations. His poem "Give Me A Chance" talks about the struggles of being a starving artist with student loans. "Since my art has done anything for me, and I would be noble and toil on, I swear I would live for the art and the art alone, and all that crap-ass, but college loans are monthly up my ass." His humorous poesy gives levity to otherwise depressing circumstances.

My goal in writing poetry is simple. I want to express myself without judgment. As a poet, I walk in my truth. I am blessed to have been built up by adversity and not destroyed despite it. For me, poetry is my solace. When writing my poems, I intend to express my feelings, especially when the words don't come easily verbally.

PREFACE

My poetry is my autobiography. I've had 48 years of life experience that lends itself to my poetic themes and prosody. I was raised by my dad who was physically abusive and drank a lot. My mom was my schizophrenic best friend who spent several years in a mental hospital, but I loved her beyond measure. By the time I was 18, I'd lost half of my family to homicide. Both of my brothers were gunned down at the age of 16, within 4 years of each other.

I first began writing poetry in 1989 when my first brother, the oldest was murdered. Counseling was an option not taken so writing became a way to communicate not just my feelings about his death, but with my brother. My brother was my protector. Although he was only sixteen when he died, he did everything in his power to make sure that I was okay. He desired to protect me, which led him to sell drugs. Standing in that knowledge made me feel guilty as if it was my fault that he was murdered. Having that cross to bear, made me determined to be an independent woman capable of fending for myself. I don't ever want someone's bad decisions to be a result of trying to help me, ever again. As time went on, I found myself writing poems about my relationships. My first relationship poem was called Front Porch Reviews.

The poem had absolutely nothing to do with the front porch, it was simply where I was sitting at the time that I wrote the poem. I remember the sun shining on the weathered front porch. I had been smitten with my new lover since childhood and we were finally in an adult relationship. That day on the front porch my views about love were anticipative and animated. That blissful emotional state spilled over into the amorous daydream poetry that ensued. Although I didn't have an understanding of the importance of titles (and probably still don't) it became obvious to me, that I could use my life experiences to create genuine, relevant poetry and prose that reflect my personal experiences.

I use my poetry as the stage for which internal cerebral conversation and soul-driven emotion find artistic asylum word and ink dance the tango to marked rhythms and abrupt pauses simile and metaphorical lines live life unique to every writer's ballpoint expression and each reader's perceptive analysis figuratively formed free verses, manipulatively malleable metered lines deliver private performances customized

for every ear and eye Outfitted in stanzas of two-line couplets openly accented in forms that articulate narratives and stories sprinkled with alliteration's consistent consonant sound descriptive imagery partners with cacophony's discordance and euphony's musicality fashion distinctive lyrics piercing thoughts and feelings, intriguing sight and sound invoking touch and taste inviting smell; It is freedom!
I use my poetry as a looking glass into "my America".

The cultural influences that breathe life into my poetry are the inner city's social and economically downtrodden people who survive and succumb to Baltimore City. I am so used to being in a survival mood, that living like that has become automatic. Automatic in the sense that I pretty much know what to expect out of my day: wake up, live, make it back home, sleep, and do it all again. It's hard to describe to someone that's not from Baltimore, or an area where there are drugs and liquor stores on every corner and gun violence is commonplace. As a resident of this fair city, I've learned to navigate through the negative so that I can make it home at the end of the day with my life and all my limbs.
Baltimore City has its urban soundtrack from the booming sounds of gunshots, buzzing

helicopters overhead, ear-piercing ambulance and police sirens blaring, at regular intervals it seems. These melodic representations of mayhem still get drowned out by kids laughing and playing, dirt bikes revving, and music blasting; a reminder of how life isn't so bad and why it's called "Charm City."

My goal in writing poetry is simple. I want to express myself without judgment. As a poet, I walk in my truth. I am blessed to have been built up by adversity and not destroyed despite it. For me, poetry is my solace. When writing my poems, I intend to express my feelings, especially when the words don't come easily verbally. Writing poetry is therapeutic for me it is my ticket to mental freedom. Ultimately, I hope that my poems can give a voice to others who may be suffering in silence.

Losing Love

How do you lose love?
Does it get lost in one of the supermarket aisles?
Attention all shoppers
Love:
Your party is waiting for you at the front exit!-
Or maybe-

Love was kidnapped.
Ransome not reads:
Pay Dearly OR Love DIES!
No further instructions were given-

How about...
Love developed Alzheimer's and forgot where it
lives
As a result,
Your best friend picked love up and took it
home-
to their house...
and forgot to let you know.

Late breaking news
This just in-
Love is Dead!!!
Be on the lookout for

"Infidelity" and
"Lack of Trust"
They are considered armed and dangerous.

They are responsible for the loss of Love.

Depression

They say you only get one true love.

What if you were lucky enough to have two?

One a soulmate who understands your hidden
insecurities

and nurtures your heart and mind as if it's their
own

the other-

a ying-yang twin

a pain in the ass

and still

the beat of your heart.

What if all of a sudden you lost them both?

Words can't begin to depict the emotional

fog I've been in since my love dearly departed.

My Cali-King has become my confidant.

isolating me from the outside noise

wrapping me in its soothing warm embrace

Leaving it, just feels wrong.

I will not;

even if I could muster the mental strength to do
so

Blackout curtains adorn the windows

Daylight seems like a distant memory.

I surrender to the cozy and comfortable
ambiance.

A façade of a peaceful retreat

Behind closed doors

In the solitary quietness

My room feels like a sanctuary of relaxation

In reality,

it's my tomb perpetuated by my depression.

Tired

Tired of waking up tired
Tired of hitting snooze on an alarm that's set too
early anyway
Tired of trying to brush your teeth and
sponge-curl your hair simultaneously
It's like rubbing your belly and patting your head
at the same time.
You're bound to miss a beat.
Tired of rushing through traffic like a bat out of
hell
to pay to park,
take that long walk,
and still arrive at work three minutes late.
Tired of being bombarded with questions before
the key unlocks the office door
Especially by those whose title is higher than
yours
There are far too many Indians and not enough
Chiefs.
Tired of meetings being called just before lunch
that run late and the boss doesn't want to
compensate.
Tired of the meeting about the meeting,
to talk about what to do about something that
does not concern you

Tired of thinking about the time they waste
doing nothing
Disguising it as something,
while your work sits
Tired of getting off at 5 but still working at 6,
 cause the meeting went too long
Or someone had a question
You couldn't answer because you were in a
meeting discussing something that turned out to
be nothing
Tired of fighting the hectic downtown traffic to
get home to find:
The house is not kept
And dinner is not cooked
Tired of eating out of containers that come in
bags that say,
"Thank You :)"
Because they know,
you'll come again
Tired of not being able to relax
There's no Calgon to "take you away"
And solace at home is D.O.A.
Unless it's payday then it's just
M.I.A.
Tired of having racing thoughts about how the
next day will start
Tired of lying down to pray
And thanking the Lord for this day
Praying-

For a better tomorrow.
No instant replay of yesterday's performance.
Waking up tired is the worst!

World of Sin

I was born into this world of sin.
At times sin was my unconditional best friend
I can remember when it all begin-
Born out of wedlock to a father who was a
rolling rock-
A mother experiencing a mental block
I was born into this world of sin.
Mice, roaches, police, and evictions.
Mental affliction is far greater than substance
addiction
"I love my babies but they driving me crazy!"

I was born into this world of sin.
Shelter homes and foster care
Beating with plastic belts,
Worm thick welts
NO one to hear my cries for help-
This is the hand that I was dealt.

I was born into this world of sin.
Sometimes sin was my only friend!
Boys and men like to show me affection
Touching and groping...
Even if they were kin to me-
Their sin was a friend to me

They were people dear to me.
They were showing they cared for me-

I was born into this world of sin.
Drunk, abusive father who wanted no bother
with a daughter
Especially a reminder of her crazy mother-
Both she and her brother
He showed more love for the brother from
another mother-
Praying for relief
Sadly, he was struck with grief.
There once were three, now there's just me.
I became an only child
And sin was still my friend.

I was born into this world of sin.
I did not ask for the life I ended up in.
Sometimes sin has been my unconditional
friend.
Lying and stealing,
Even sexual healing has helped to make my
feelings less revealing
"Hurt you, before you hurt me" is what I say
But in the end, I'm the one who pays.

I was born into this world of sin
But that doesn't mean I have to "fit in"
And sin-

Is not my FRIEND!
It is time to let go
and let God into this world of sin I was born in.

The Cost of Love

At what price do we pay for love?
Do we succumb to pain in order for love to
remain?
Disregarding all disdain-
Attempting to hide the pain.
In the end, what do we gain?

At what cost do we engulf ourselves in love?
To no avail,
We blind ourselves to problems
Searching desperately for solutions
For resolutions.
Hoping,
it won't be a means to an end
Trying helplessly to amend.

What charge do we accept for love?
Do we offer our heart to 'foot the bill' or,
Give our soul in return for a chance to maybe...
Caress?
Hold?
Thinking, maybe love will lighten the load
We anxiously welcome love into our abode.

Who picks up the tab when love is no more?

All that remains,
                Aborted promises
                  Abused Feelings
                    Months of intense
emotional healing.

Who pays for the misdealings?
Who mends the hurt feelings?
At what price do we pay for love?

The Henderson's

In sickness and in health
Check!
We cornered that.
Sometimes it seemed like the bad days
outweighed the good
But every time we got through it
Together-
My support,
your fight,
Our Love!
A love that has no borders.
No resemblance to normal
Pure-
Unconditional love.
Selfless!
Forgiving!
Forehead kisses-
Mr. and Mrs...
Till Death Do US Part
Never!
You live in my heart.
In this life and the next-
You are my first and forever
I Do!
My endless love,
Forever your Beloved!

Living and Dying

15

Living is hard to do
when your dead on the inside.
Trying hard not to show the outside
A Gemini mentality perceives this reality
Introverted psychology masked with,
"I'm Okay"
Silently drowning in the memories
of lost lives and aborted dreams.
Things aren't ever what they seem.
Dying is hard to do,
when you're fighting to live on the inside!

June 28th

Cloudy gray pupils
Stare straight ahead with no focal point
Black bile ooze like deadly lava
from the mouth
moisture-kissed skin unmoving
No pulse.
No. Heart. Beat.
Lifeless in a claret lounger
Delore Pearman Lindsay
Died in her sleep
June 28, 2010,
I lost my best friend.

Contemplating Death

Will you forgive me?
I am tired
and time is unwinding
two-for-one drink specials parlayed into slurred,
"I Love you"
Drunken text
      Anchors to the past for years to come.

Will you forgive me?
I am sad
and perpetually plagued by life-extinguished
Tony McLean inhumanly exterminated by an
unseen shadow in the night
      Misguided souls in calamity and turmoil

Will you forgive me?
I have tried
And no one hears me
Loud silence occupies my space
      Sinking into unquiet contemplations

Will you forgive me
when
      I am gone-

Who Pulled the Trigger

Who pulled the trigger that changed a life
That paralyzed a spine and crippled a mind-
Black Lives don't matter as plasma pools on
black asphalt
With Facebook Live black genocide is televised
like Revolutions
Stop Snitchin' cultivate disappeared bodies
reappearing decapitated, mutilated, maimed
unable to be claimed

Photoshopped club pics adorned with Angel
wings
sympathetic Eulogies to Street Kings reference
imploded street dreams of THOTs and glocks,
singin' fuck da cops' while slingin' rocks
Elicit Momma's piercing screams
He was a good boy.
He loved his family.
He WOULD not hurt anybody.
A mother's dream deferred
further by camouflaged lies
Lies become truth when grieving
Even when the truth is there to see
Life Changed.

Why would Black Lives Matter
when life doesn't matter to black lives.
Black lives get dismantled by black hands like
earthquakes
destroy building foundations
Closed caskets display death's dedication to
living
while the Pastor celebrates a lifeless life
without air or substance,
well spent-
Who pulled the trigger that took my life?

Grieving Love's Playlist

'Last night a DJ Saved My Life'
with "Another Sad Love Song'
on this 'Heartbreak Anniversary'
while 'Reminiscing'
on 'Days Gone By'

We were' Crazy In Love'
Riding the "love Rollercoaster'
'The First Time Ever I Saw Your Face'
I thought, 'At Last'
I found my 'Dream Lover'
And with you,
I felt, ' The Greatest Love of all"
Now I find myself 'Dancing on My Own'

"Losing You" demolished me like a 'Wrecking
Ball'
I 'Could Cry Just Thinking about you'
You left me 'All by Myself'
No 'Last Kiss'
No goodbye.
Just, 'Caught Out There'
'Rolling in the Deep' like a 'Candle in the Wind'

'Since You Been Gone'
It's been ' A Darker kind of Day'

Coupled with 'Lonely Nights'
I'm 'Hurt'

'The Drugs Don't Work" on grief pain.
Even in my sleep,
I search for a 'Glimpse of Us'
The Scent of you...
The old me...
'I Remember'
'When We Were Young'
Thinking we had ' A Couple of Forevers'
It just 'Slipped Away'

In sleep, 'How I weep'
and then, it's 'Back to Black'

'Gone Too Soon'
'A Part of Me' still grieves for you.
Memories of you 'Linger' like smoke in the air.
I wish I knew ' How to Save a Life'
But 'Heaven Was Needing a Hero'

'My Immortal'
'I Will Always Love You'
In this life and the next; 'To Where You Are'

I'll keep 'Dreaming with a Broken Heart'
and pray you see my 'Tears in Heaven'
'In Loving Memory' of my Two Lost Loves.

Poetic Inspiration

I digress into turmoil and
bitterness
An empty page holds the lines in which my
sins are depicted.
Devotion of LOVE-
Adoration of LUST
Construct beautiful vivid pictures with
words
embodying the makings of me!

It is from MY HEART,
MY LIFE.
MY PEN,
Where my writing begins and end.

Commode

Naked walls gaze back at me
offering no solace
Only comforting solitude
Constipated spigots wait quietly to release.
Thoughts about dieting churn ideas like diarrhea
Guts bubble like a volcanic eruption
In the quiet,
the bouquet of excremental lava
infuses with a flowery essence
Deep contemplation reveals silent elation

Sitting in the quiet
daydreaming about nightmares-
pondering how to get out of debt
wondering how to live without regret

Naked walls gaze back at me
In the quiet, without interruption
I meditate upon the commode

Infidelity

Is it the gray hint or hazel tint of your eyes
Your indulgent sweet skin
that disguise your lies
As you confess your love-soaked sin

Craving the balminess of your breath on my
innermost being
Anticipating this passionate iniquity
Contrived arguments host opportunities for
carnal sightseeing
Clandestine Rendezvous hides the obliquity

Vows made in love lay sundered by lust
Adoring affairs altered with an acceptance of
being alone
Mentally eulogizing nuptials overdosed on
mistrust, buried like ashes returned to dust
Reincarnation of a friend as lover enthrone

Matrimony was a promise made between two
That was until I met you.

Without Love

25

If I could live without love
I'd silence my beating beacon
to avoid Cupid's detection.
Shrink wrap my heart to muffle
the sound,
store it in bubble wrap
to protect its fragile feelings.
Then wait patiently-

If I could live without love
I'd place it in an airtight coffin
sealed securely with secrets and sadness.
Bind it with precautionary mistrust
and infidelity tape.
Bury it underneath the
broken and tattered floorboards of life.
Then patiently wait-
for love's resurrection.

Relationship Double Talk

Anticipating your arrival

the ticking counts down the minutes

Waiting for you.

even when hating you

I never regret dating you.

Like football Sunday, this is a game

you play

and yet,

forever in my heart, you stay

Like high cholesterol, you

harm my heart

tracking your sludge in and out of

my life

Your wants are a mystery

Your taunts are my misery.

I'm not mad that you didn't show.

I've realized with that blow.

You and I are at the close of our

show.

I Bet

I bet he wishes he heard the car alarm chirp
or the wooden deck
crackle under the pressure
of her heavy feet as she approached the door

I bet he wishes he locked the lock and there was
no key

I bet he wishes I didn't turn the knob to open that
door
or hear her moans soaring above the Spanish
version of Wolverine
drowning in the background

I bet I wish I didn't see
that strange woman
with your familiar dick
in her mouth

I bet I wish I didn't see
her naked brown ass grinding
as she fucked the air

I bet y'all wish I didn't grab that broom
and you didn't feel the cool breeze

just before
the metal came crashing down
against y'all naked flesh.

Party over Bitches!

I bet she didn't think she'd end up on the porch
butt ass naked
crying for her clothes
Pleading to that man's
Wife
In the middle of the night

I bet she didn't know she would change his life.

I bet he didn't think he'd get caught
or he'd be on the outside looking in
I bet he didn't know he would lose a good friend

I bet they both knew
there was nothing left to do

I bet no sad apologies whispered
will be excepted
and fingers snapping to point the blame
Rejected!

I bet our marriage was defamed,
I bet things will never be the same.

and
I bet this is, Match, Set, Game!

Alternate Reality

I love the smell of your cologne that reminds me
of Christmas pine.
Until you drown in it.
You love the taste of the salty unbathed nape of
my neck.
And have the nerve to say, 'You smell good.'
I love your ebony skin that fills like silk gliding
against my skin.
As it crawls…
Mentally trying to psych me up for what LIES
ahead.
You love to trace the rounds of my cheeks with
your semi-soft callused fingers.
Wash your damn hands...
bacteria, and germs.
Always my concern
You loved it when I kissed your thin paper chip
lips.
I hate when you try to kiss me
your breath smells like shit.
You love it when I climb on top
I hate you can't work the space between my
thighs.
My sounds of ecstasy...LIES.
You think you give 'Big Dick' Energy.

Your micro penis is like a pinky inside me.
You love fucking me and going 'balls deep"
this must be your reality in your sleep
I hate faking like I enjoy you.
bouncing inside my play house
your penis is too short for the ride.
If sexual pleasure was a course,
You'd fail.
You can't even finger-fiddle the middle properly.
I extremely dislike the fact; that your oral sex
feels like a cat licking me.
Or a finger nub tickling the sensual side of my
ivory
Your tiny mouth harbors saliva that reeks of
sewage.
Your tongue is as petite as a snail without its
shell.
Your man meat is miniature like a chocolate
Tootsie Roll.
Me and You…
We're in the same bed
but our experience is not the same...
You love our sex and I hate it!

Loss of Life

You are breaking me.
with the
continual lies and sneaking about

Making me delusional,
Playing head and heart games
victimizing my manhood with your control

You got your hooks in me,
your smell,
your feel,
your taste…
It disturbs me to think
someone else is eating your cake,
Deceitful whore…

Bitch you caught red-handed,
Fucking dudes where I lay my head…
Disrespect won't be tolerated.
I gotta get my shit and go…
Go-
I can't leave,
I gotta think…
No financial stability, no family support,
feeling stuck…

I can't sleep,
Difficulty concentrating… thoughts racing,
Racing-

I hear you calling me
delusional…
delusional...

The echo of your voice resides in my head…
Pacing the floor, palms getting sweaty, heart
beating faster,
Faster-

Feeling sick to my stomach
trembling…
I gotta get out of here!
Gotta get out-

You slide out of the car panty-less,
snapped…
Zapped...

Like your red lipstick-stained lips-
red blood pours…
Blood pours

Hashtag

#ComplyorDie
Nobody move!
Nobody get shot by cop
Orlando Castille felt the heat
of that nervous cop's glock
Hear his fiancé scream-
See his blood stream,
on the computer screen
Losing life live.

#ComplyorDie
Get
d
  o
    w
      n
on the ground!

Wrestle mania on concrete sidewalks
single Black man versus cops
Eric Garner, "I can't breathe"
on repeat, he screams,
"I can't breathe!"
Choked until he couldn't speak.

Another black man living,
lost life in the street.

#ComplyorDie

Hands

        p
     u

in the air!

Alone on a traffic-less highway
police feet engage on the ground
while their eye in the sky surveille
the "bad dude"
Terence Crutcher felt the zing of the Taser sting
six seconds later,
he heard the gun sing
"Shots fired" the radio blared!
He looked like a "bad dude"
And yet...
I care!

#ComplyorDie

Resilient(Found Poem)

37

You are great.No matter where others pretend
that you rate
to overcome a challenge in life...
figure out how what was once out of sight,
living only in a dream,
becomes a reality, here to be seen
Life's full of corners, valleys, and hills
see them as thrills
an absolute miracle, how most of them thrive
alters our perspective
and repels
or appeals
how we feel.
Be genuine, authentic and true,
about who's really you.
You are capable;
durable,
adaptable and strong.
To suggest otherwise is quite simply-
Wrong.

www.ingramcontent.com/pod-product-compliance
Lightning Source LLC
La Vergne TN
LVHW021307200726